"This book is the answer to your question: Am I not worthy of love just because I'm cruel and disgusting? It's for those of us who deeply understand that everything has a price, including us, our souls, and each of our body parts. Not because we want it that way, but because you, you who are reading this, have made clear to us, for our entire lives, that our bodies and love and voices are objects with respective values. An all-consuming anger had me devouring this book in one sitting. And the book devoured me. We burned together."

—MITSKI

"Jenny Zhang will always be one of the most important poets writing today. She consistently and constantly stretches the lyric to its necessary and best intentions, telling it where it only may dream or dare to go. In *My Baby First Birthday*, she grapples with the very essence of being, how caustic and necessary it is to exist, how cruel the world is with little remorse or self-reflection, and how painful and glorious it can be to 'flick[] cum out/beautiful white globs that dry mid-air.' Throughout all of its bleak conclusions about the present, *My Baby First Birthday* provides immense hope, too. For it was when we were babies—and almost just simply ideas—that we felt real and unconditional love. Perhaps, these poems suggest, we can exist in this welcoming space again one day, if we recognize our faults as humans (of which there are many) and correctly worship our delicious brutality and appeal. Perhaps, this book says, it's the human instinct in us to dream that gives us the greatest possibility of a healthy future. Dream, Zhang implores here. And we do."

—DOROTHEA LASKY, AUTHOR OF *MILK*

"*My Baby First Birthday* is like performing when you suspect someone is watching vs when you hope someone will pay attention. It's viscous, oozing with anger and humor and sexy sexy death. I love how it opens and opens and opens itself, exasperated by the world history of contradiction & inequality—yet, despite itself, retains a tender, caring core. This book is literally breathtaking. By the end I had to remind myself to breathe."

—TOMMY PICO, AUTHOR OF *FEED*

"Rabelais wrote *Gargantua and Pantagruel* and Jenny Zhang wrote *My Baby First Birthday*, a marvelous book full of cunts, puke, farting oceans, and seppuku, which amounts to an accuracy of feeling. I will probably get in trouble for putting Rabelais in a blurb because almost nobody reads old books or really any books. Jenny Zhang makes me feel alive. Her rage and appetites are unslakable. If everything feels stupid and wrong to you, congratulations: read this book."

—ARIANA REINES, AUTHOR OF *A SAND BOOK*

PRAISE FOR *SOUR HEART*

Winner of the PEN/Robert W. Bingham Prize for Debut Fiction
and the L.A. Times Art Seidenbaum Award for First Fiction,
and named a best book of the year by *The New Yorker*;
NPR; *O, The Oprah Magazine*; *The Guardian*; *Esquire*;
New York; and BuzzFeed

"[Jenny Zhang's] coming-of-age tales are coarse
and funny, sweet and sour, told in language that's
rough-hewn yet pulsating with energy."

—*USA TODAY*

"One of the knockout fiction debuts of the year."

—*NEW YORK*

"Compelling writing about what it means to be a teenager . . .
It's brilliant, it's dark, but it's also humorous and filled with love."

—ISAAC FITZGERALD, *TODAY*

"A combustible collection . . . in a class of its own."

—BOOKLIST (STARRED REVIEW)

"Gorgeous and grotesque . . . [a] tremendous debut."

—*SLATE*

MY BABY
FIRST BIRTHDAY

MY BABY
FIRST BIRTHDAY

JENNY ZHANG

 TIN HOUSE BOOKS / Portland, Oregon

Published by Tin House Books, Portland, Oregon

Distributed by W. W. Norton & Company

Library of Congress Cataloging-in-Publication Data

Names: Zhang, Jenny, author.
Title: My baby first birthday / Jenny Zhang.
Description: Portland, Oregon : Tin House Books, [2020]
Identifiers: LCCN 2020000721 | ISBN 9781947793811 (paperback) |
  ISBN 9781947793910 (ebook)
Subjects: LCGFT: Poetry.
Classification: LCC PS3626.H36 M9 2020 | DDC 811/.6—dc23
LC record available at https://lccn.loc.gov/2020000721

First US Edition 2020
Printed in the USA
Interior design by Jakob Vala

www.tinhouse.com

for my friends

CONTENTS

FALL

I keep thinking there is an august · 3

summer solstice · 5

My baby first birthday · 6

everything is scary but yr love is good · 10

Flush in the spirals of black holes · 11

bad day · 12

your whole body is slanted · 13

needs revision! · 15

what is with you · 21

jenny's theme / walk away and embrace · 22

Could I ever? · 23

we were lonelier in there · 25

what a terrible ****!!! · 28

same lesson over and over again forever · 29

leetle · 30

jenny's theme / have to accept · 32

DREAMS / SO BRIGHT OUTSIDE I CAN'T SEE · 33

it is so lonely to be strong · 35

it was terrible to hear the leaves · 36

THE LAST FIVE CENTURIES WERE UNEVENTFUL · 38

WINTER

My baby first birthday · 43

ted talk · 45

ariana's theme · 47

becoming a person was easy · 48

don't you get it · 49

seppuku · 50

little tea party at home · 52

uncle boo · 55

jenny's trying · 56

The Universal Energy Is About to Intervene in Your Life · 57

castles in the air for the very very · 60

yeast · 62

You are the poorest person here · 63

my sword · 65

My baby first birthday · 66

ariana's theme (reprise) · 67

Natural · 68

ymca · 69

suddenly I'm so hungry · 72

Ell · 73

"revision" · 75

there is only world · 76

jenny's trying (reprise) · 78

with my mother in nice · 79

goo goo water · 81

SPRING

Everyone's girlfriend · 85

it's spring · 87

screenshot for later · 89

It was a period when cunt was in the air · 90

HAMMER · 92

it's so intoxicating to be unwell · 97

NO · 98

THERE IS NOTHING TO SAY · 99

spring discourse · 101

I feel nothing but hatred hatred hatred hatred · 102

it brought you · 103

Don't · 104

Is it possible for me to become the person
you love the most in your life · 106

tanaïs's theme · 108

I had a lot to say · 109

why would you ever be friends with her? · 111

Groupon · 113

Fidget · 114

jenny's trying / victoria's theme · 117

Someone · 118

remember / it brought you (reprise) · 119

Aegean · 120

SUMMER

your pubes are everywhere · 125

Great · 127

brittani's theme · 129

dumb theory · 130

I know others before me have been this way · 132

I'm a 30 year old White non racist male, with some of my closest friends being Black. With that being said · 133

I will go for forty five minutes · 138

from the dead dark into the green · 140

We must rapidly begin · 142

It is finally midsummer · 144

the morning of yesterday's yesterday is for once soft · 146

I have to · 147

I would have no pubes if I were truly in love · 148

shamepuff · 153

communication ≠ connection · 155

worried · 157

I didn't know better · 158

which is why I am telling you about this now · 161

A troll · 162

haha hey · 165

Baby's first birthday · 167

Instant Classic · 170

a little life / everyone's theme · 172

The natural sunlight goes away · 173

Is there a way to drain a lake you are afraid
you will one day drown in? · 175

why do we have to all be someone · 178

volition · 179

under the chiming bell · 180

YOUR PROBLEMS · 182

IT WAS SO BRIGHT I COULD NOT SEE · 184

FALL

I keep thinking there is an august

if there is an august
there is an august
I would probably write every day
but some days I get caught up
rubbing my pussy
checking for pimples
green ones pop on their own
when I need to cum
or when I'm flicking cum out
beautiful white globs that dry mid-air
I would be lazier than this
but then it would be
celestial
a star in midsummer
summer solstice long gone
the weird feeling of being alone
of consummating love
why do my friends look forward
to the best day of their lives
do they secretly wish
they were already dead?
do I?
does he?

do all of us
already know something
of death
the next life
the old world
in the old country
they ate the horses they rode on
and no one said anything stupid
like how life is both impossible
and happening at the same time
no one spoke thru the ground to touch
- god -
but that was the old country
where my mother is from
where you're from
your mother studied my mother
your recreational sports came from our rivers
your houses were decorated
with objects so rare my people have only heard about them
in songs passed down by the one family member who befriended
a European traveler
whyyyyyyyyyyyyyyyyyyyyyyyyyyyyyy me
yr people cried
while visiting the old country
where I have never been
the place where I was first touched
a sudden bloom of algae
in the ancient lake
where all the animals touched skin to skin fur to fur paw to paw fin
    to fin mouth to mouth hole to hole and became family

summer solstice

will be significant
im going to release something
soft and radiant
and true
into the world

My baby first birthday

say something say something
if you see something say something
H1N1
each one teach one
because of avian flu my stupid cunt cousin
could not get an education
on your stupid cunt shores
where my mother sold her house
to give me a stupid cunt education
where I learned about social entrepreneurship
that it is a good thing
to give pencils to mothers
who are incarcerated
they can take those pencils and break them
in their stupid cunts
I bail out every one of those cunts
for ten grand a pop
they run rampant
like you fucking know what it's like
my detachable pussy is not afraid of being
approached by a man late at night
who is like hey girl
you don't need none of that

you look good without makeup
and I feel very sexy
because my cunt gets leashed to a tree
and waves hello to everyone
like hi like hi like hi hi hi
each one teach one
I teach each one to have one more
so in case this cunt dies
I have another
in case this man marries me
I can still fuck
I can still go to jail for fucking
I can still go to jail for not fucking
I can still go to jail and have it all
and have nothing
and wake up to my detached body intact
in this way you are never alone
in this way you are never translated
I said to say stop if you speak chinese
but it's worse to be visible than it is to be invisible
you see me and then tell my friend
she looks exactly like me
well she looks exactly like me
because she is me
and I'm also me
and I'm visible ya cunt
I'm miserable ya hero
I'm miserable and I speak perfect English
on the phone you agree

in person you ask me where I'm from *originally*
I seppuku on the spot and you are like
OK STOP
and I am like OKAY I STOPPED
and like there's no more
and like there's just that now
and like I am totally fine
and like I am gonna do it again
and like your poetry gives me a motherly halo
and like I am gonna have babies and get someone else to look after them
and like I'm dead but you won't stop
until my cunt re-attaches itself to my body
and that's when I will cease to go outside
and that's when I will cease to fear anything
you walk like a hero and I praise you
in front of my family
the only ones who know me
and I don't have time for less thoughts
more slowly
more meaning
less quickly
I am running to catch the bus
my cunt makes it
of course
but me
I am tired
I am out of breath
lying on a map
and the city where I was born

disappears mysteriously
like anyway I know who did it
I will praise him in front of his family
who have never seen him chase after a bus
full of cunts
like I have
who will never know him
like I do
like I know
like I know
like I know

everything is scary but yr love is good

goo goo baby
sweet baby
be the baby ppl didn't let u be
for once in yr life
& see what happens

Flush in the spirals of black holes

you didn't just want to puke in your mother's mouth you wanted her to feel as big and lonesome as the puke that did not want you if it wanted you wouldn't it have stayed inside wouldn't it have said hi and been more reasonable and less lonely and less afraid of the sun and of drying in your hands where it was born alive and wet and not inside but you wanted to expel it like you want to expel things that have nowhere to go like I am someone who has no where to go no mother to live inside like your mother does not live inside her mother so what now like every mother has to live separately and your puke has to live outdoors and we have to live like children live never knowing how to be mothers or fathers never wanting our families to die so we don't have to start our own and then the world can be puked on by a different world and the universe is the wide open mouth we live inside the puked-on stars and the puked-on asteroids and the puke riding on the backs of comets saying wooooooooo and the puke swirling flush in the spirals of black holes is like woooooooooooo and we are like woooooooooooooo you and I stand in your puke and I hold your hand and you tell me you don't recognize me at all and I want to be those comets and those asteroids and strap you onto a rock and fall through space forever puking into the endlessness that does not know its own infinity or anything at all, really!

bad day

i cut my hair
then paid again
to cut more hairs
then paid more
to cut again
then again i paid
again i cut
i cut and paid and cut and paid
still so ugly
I cud die
it's not fair
ppl who are already loved
are the best candidates
for more love
while ppl in mortal danger
try to dodge
all the saviors
who wanna make heroes
out of our peril

your whole body is slanted

why did you touch me there
between my fingers
"it feels like a mountain range"
well I'm very sick these days
I keep telling my friends I'm not
a liberal not a conservative
what are you then?
I can be traced back to the tiny dancer
Flaubert loved; he was pedestrian
other canonical men knew my mother
painted her so wrong did not know
how a nose like hers really looked in profile
I was seven then eight then nine then dead
what I would give to not be read
as a means of instruction
when did I agree to be a textbook
for you and your whole dumb family
my people make history if they just stay alive
well anything is easy if yr existence is wanted
admit you want me to have a function
admit you can't imagine someone
touching you the way you touch me
you don't like being bought or sold

and what I must tolerate
you have never
ever

needs revision!

I liked the story of the monkey
who was inside
that woman and when she met
that man
who fucked her without asking
about pain or pleasure or desire or terror
he was really fucking
the monkey inside her
who told her to stop
if only we all had a monkey
but actually ~ no ~
no to wanting someone else
to do the work for us
no to wanting someone to feel
our pain
no to thinking everything can be
outsourced
someone has to feel it
it might as well be me
just because I have let monsters
love me shouldn't mean I get to
hit whoever I want
and ~ yes ~ I want to hit everyone!

walk around with my fists by my side
like a spring I knock down everything
around me
the horror is always the same:
what fell were the flowers
leaving just the ragged hedges
the immovable trunks of trees
everything ugly remains
the bleeding is just on one side
the same people care
and the same people don't
I don't know man . . . was I wrong
to assume I was straight?
what else was in me all along that I never nurtured?
I point out sadist after sadist
but don't know how to look at myself
well all around us are people who don't know
until someone calls for a boycott
and someone else with no disposable income
promises publicly they won't spend it

~

I honestly don't know
how to scare the fuck out of him—
he has too much money to care
it sucks that even white girls can't get justice
and the rest of us are supposed to keep writing
about the time someone put their hand up our legs

the time someone put something else up something else
it's just holes it's just ugly appendages
it's just an orifice
it's just someone's entire history of violence
it's just going dead inside for one to seven minutes
it's just sleeping in unwanted sperm
it's just someone's parent who *knows* their son
    & he would *never* never hurt anyone
it's just marrying someone who has offshore accounts
in the Seychelles and using bitcoins to buy more land in Puerto Rico
it's just writing on instagram: "best decision I ever made
marrying this one"
now no one is afraid to get drinks with "this one"
he's "safe" because he married a nerd who thinks
she's a 19th century aristocrat
everyone with secret wealth
publicly fetishizes rich people's ideas of thrift
it sucks I'm too violent to be praised
by actually powerful people
they prefer the dummies who feel
sorry for all the Roman Polanski films
they can't stream anymore
on moral grounds
they'll only retweet that article about
how women are monsters too
I mean get fucking real
did someone with this level of professional achievement
actually agonize for three weeks
over watching that scene in Annie Hall

where Diane Keaton cucks Woody Allen
so gracefully and deceptively?
I once saw a group of future
Men Going Their Own Ways
actually praise the movie as if it weren't
the nightmare they wrote their manifestos against

~

#goals for a white supremacy that outlaws
any dick stiffening outside a vagina
the followers of thor's hammer can't get enough
of these sideways asian cunts
they worship odin
but can't get hard unless there's a chink around
I guess it's true women are so powerful
that a single drop of cum landing anywhere
but inside our wombs would destroy western civ
can anyone resolve then how
a single drop of unwanted cum
can make my friends and I actual survivors?
I would never call myself a survivor
just because that skinny little pencil dick
went in and then fell out
~ too skinny ~ I screamed
it hurts all the more
thanks to all the unused surface area
how did both of us come away from that
thinking each other was the nazi

~

when I was fourteen I actually prayed
for someone to rape me
how was I supposed to know
what that word meant
how it would actually feel
it was the fastest route to attention
all the other ways I was broken
didn't ~ count ~
how was I supposed to know
nothing counts if you're a woman in pain
how was I supposed to know
the more I talk about my pain
the more white people literally profit
how was I supposed to know then
I was already eroticizing my trauma
in order to seem luckier than the girls I knew
who talked in terms of disfigurement
are there any women left
who haven't cried on tape?
every time I say something
a man I've never thought about even once in my life
lets me know how it makes him feel
this is one of the best strategies
to get me to think about you
what a fucking prison it is
to be inside this femme mind
I wish it could end right here

but actually pessimism is more than sane
this body has never been touched consensually
are you kidding me???
exploitation doesn't stop just because
I started doing mad push-ups
and worked on my core
I hate this reality but neither
will I just die
I will live okay
I will bite my tongue until it's gone
not to make any kind of point
though it is true one way
to seize the means of production
might be self-mutilation
might be suicide without a note
no warnings on facebook
no threats on twitter
just go away
let the paper write an obituary
for someone who resembles you
the dead don't laugh
they don't applaud heroic acts
they don't have unfinished business
they aren't salvation for the living
they are dead dead dead
& deserve
at least
some rest

what is with you

and your need to not ever be blamed?

jenny's theme / walk away and embrace

the unknown
as scary and lonely as it is

Could I ever?

all the world doesn't care
don't you ever
take your mouth off my page
I scroll thru pages and pages of text
honestly never thought
you could never
in china xi is left but once my vpn loads
I see not so in my news apps
what's the chinkie word for tankies
I wonder if mao really cared about the third world
his followers to this day
still really hate dark skin
in my family women get gifted facekinis
and offered double eyelid surgery
my grandparents liberated shanghai
took over the french concession
stoned the landlords
and distributed land to the people!
seventy years later they still reside there
the park avenue of shanghai
the upper east side of the East
I was given too much and have fought too little
even my chinese blood has outlived its purpose

is it dumb to care
or is it right to ask questions
eye dee kay and eye dee cee
I say for the digital archives
in the library of congress
but surely you know me
more than that

we were lonelier in there

my father loved a thick thigh
my mother smashed both of hers
in the old meatpacking district
squiggles of raw meat
vacuum sealed
I swear to god I squealed
when someone with my eyes
triple lutzed in the air
I noticed that beautiful leg
smeared with the same glittery lotion
stealing from bath and body works
is truly an art
if yr a white girl
if yr a white girl
anything goes
I noticed Kristi Yamaguchi was acceptable
Tonya Harding was not
Nancy Kerrigan was actually working class
they made her stand next to Mickey
"so dumb . . . I hate it"
she drank Campbell's chicken noodle soup
with a very shallow spoon
that too

is a white girl thing
the utter loneliness of the whole world
as expressed by the endless infinity of whatever
is just a girl thing I think
I haven't met someone who was pro Betty
anti Veronica
or someone who thought
Archie was actually fuckable
guess I knew you were an all lowercase kind of guy
not really into the spotlight
being anti
means getting lotsa praise
I have nothing—
only good things to say about you
on the ice and in the thin cold air
I keep giving good leg
imitating my heroes
liking them more and more
the older I get the more I'm never sad
I don't think it's just because I had a childhood
or because there was always someone around to love
there was no getting away
from a face that didn't deserve it
the elders said no to ice rinks
lifetime movies starting with blood
"did anyone love her? did anyone stop her?"
what was there to see anyway
little girls waving hello and the flags of all my countries
waving back

all who live with heat
beaming just beaming
"She was a semi-celebrity who,
if she couldn't skate,
probably would have been saying,
'that's $11.50 please. Pull up
to the window for your burger and fries.'"
I honestly didn't know any white girls
who hated each other
more than they hated me
that was how little I knew
usually the ones on instagram
who say #squad
need to
the gangster we're all looking for—
lay tay dm tway
try to move your tongue as long as your leg:
lay tee yim twee

what a terrible ****!!!

is that really why
are you actually scared
or are you just
reluctant
for some reason
name him
who is he

　　　　　　　　to me the whole problem
　　　　　　　　is men don't get involved
　　　　　　　　all the people talking are women

so will you say his name or not

　　　　　　　　will you help us or not

same lesson over and over again forever

you are going to have to
let go of yr need
to control everything

leetle

in some old world
I- I- I- I always got my finger stuck
in the tiny one person pots
it was goopy and calming and obviously
flirtatious
not that ancient pain
doesn't have its own erotica
come here baby you say and stick yours
in my wet mouth and we are truly
making it
not that
it stopped hurting
bc of it

if nothing is insignificant
why doesn't anyone do anything
the best people still don't
dance cuter than when they were kids
there's a way of moving that indicates
no one has ever hurt you
and there's a way of moving
that just reeks

well if you are going to love me
you are going to have to write me
in my baby language
my other tongue did not just develop
spontaneously—
it had to be nurtured
you know that
and anyway
you might be some kind of big baby
and yr goo goo is probably gonna hurt me

still there's no question
I want this
& I want you

why meeeeeeeeeeeeeeeee
we moaned like a couple of patients
in the dead of the night
it is true we both lost respect
still
it is best to know you
best to not go back
best if you take off yr shirt
and show me yr chest
I go wowowowowowow
you go wowowowowowowow?
and I go wowowowowowowowwww!
and we go crystal clear
falling crazily through

jenny's theme / have to accept

real emotions
as overwhelming
& frightening as they are

DREAMS / SO BRIGHT OUTSIDE I CAN'T SEE

what would happen if we started labeling

                    I swear I never used to

peel

                    like this
                    three sheets slipped

under the kingdom of god

if the goddess brought u here

            why do u know so little
                why do u drop pebbles for the way back
          I don't really know
        who will survive in America

we shall have everything we want

                    and what about the

dying

                    you showed me my

origins

                    now I show you mine
                    in the deep tropics

                                        I finally sweated
                                        went glug glug glug
                                        on that dotted line
                                        your father drew
                                        the maps won't change
                                        the cities won't suffer

another name
                                        our fathers will never
again
                    fight old wars
                                        let me rest and drink
from the   of
                                        let me talk to you
without points

I said I would know you forever
                                I said we could go on and then go on
and then
                                someday even grow
                    very soft
                                                together

it is so lonely to be strong

+ no one wants to fucking hear it

it was terrible to hear the leaves

it was terrible to hear the leaves
the cold was terrible
the wind rustling was terrible
the footprints soft and dewy,
terrible,
all of it,
terrible
I have known a softer world
a dewier world
real frost
I have been so soft
skin on skin was nothing like
flesh on flesh
a cuteness not so praiseworthy
I guess I am lonely still
lonely no matter where
lonely no matter what
this is how I was before
and how I am still
it doesn't matter
. . . does it?
I live
anyway

with the loneliness
with the terrible leaves and the terrible
soft
dew

THE LAST FIVE CENTURIES WERE UNEVENTFUL

The last five centuries were uneventful
the stitches that melted
from my ripped open cunt
tasted like mint and changed color
when I peed
I peed with the door open
because this is bounty
the universe has a fat lip
we put every cock from China
inside it and splash
in the slippery oriental jizz
you feel like seppukuing because your butthole is unretractable
you feel like seppukuing because your butthole is too determined
you feel like seppukuing because one time a man was rejected by a woman
she said, You're creepy
and he got a gun
and wrote a manifesto
against bikram yoga
against women with great bodies
against women who want to have babies with other men
against women who want to have babies with men who are not allowed
    to be part of their lives after they have the baby

against women who know they are good looking
against women who have died for knowing they are good looking
against women who loved women and mocked men for jerking off
    to the idea of a woman touching a woman
I have jerked off to the idea of a man
jerking off to the idea of a woman touching a woman
and that idea bought a samurai sword from ebay
and seppukued
I wanted to have a baby
I wanted to carry my baby to term
I wanted to have milk oozing from my tits
I wanted to have bigger tits than the tits I have now
I wanted to drink my own milk and breastfeed myself
I wanted to breastfeed my mother and tell her I love her
I wanted to miscarry a baby by falling down the stairs
I wanted to toast to my own miscarriage with breast milk from my tits
I wanted to have bigger tits without having a baby
I wanted you to tell me I'm the reason why the world is going to hell
I wanted to give you the hell you said I was capable of creating
no one really cares but you do and I do
we take the relics of entire countries
and trash them in the sea
when we dive for the past
we find unearthed thoughts
the fertility of what you think could one day be
is just the honest desire to be remembered after you're dead
so much that you focus on how to be great
so much that you focus on how to be new
so much that you forget to love your father

so much that you forget to love your mother
so much that you forget to love your children
so much that you forget to love your pets
so much that you would forsake the barren godforsaken twice
farted sea which gave rise to the queen and her queenly farts
and her princely kingdom
where she once told you and I to fear everything
and we did
and we lived like that
and we still live like that
and we still know nothing
hiding our big dreams in the invisible centers of roses
where we feel big and round and ready
and ready
and ready
and ready
and ready
and ready
and ready
I'm ready
I'm ready
I'm ready
I'm ready
I'm ready
I'm ready
I'm ready

WINTER

My baby first birthday

my mother had two vaginas
one to birth me and one to keep me
inside the first one I had two names
my given name and my other given name
my twat had a name too
it was forgotten because the climate changed
the climate changed because of God
obviously
we as a society
stopped naming our twats
the old ways make way
for some way of being again
in this world where we bury the old
inside their baby bodies
this way when we wake up from our dead sleep
we shall be little bright stars
dead to the world and dead to the love
our teeny tiny gods created
their cunts hugging *so tenderly* at the moment of creation
that I think this world was truly made for us
still we won't live forever
we won't know how to tell the others
who will have surely lived like we lived

inside the total darkness of their mothers too
where it doesn't matter what we know and what we do not

ted talk

money will build anywhere
there's a view or a coastline
all those tangled shrubs and thorny bushes
your ancestors cut through centuries ago
to claim in the name of a queen
and a king with foul smelling hair
these days even the ecotone
between the living and the dying
has to be privatized & sold at auction
all the steps between next year
and the first human year ever recorded
melted so flagrantly it became stylish to be poetic
for the end of the world
everyone's collecting coins on every interface
a thousand identical posts about 2019
being the year of paper straws
and reusable cups
indigo dyeing in Kyoto
is the new 36 hours in Tbilisi
all the people with phones
don't think twice about buying onboard wifi
on their way to the latest Caribbean island
still recovering from last year's hurricanes

would it be so wrong to wish
everyone with global entry be grounded
until extinction is off the table
I don't think I can date another
digital nomad or a normie with a dog
who doesn't know what it's like
to be too poor to buy their way
out of disaster
why do the rich treat blame
like it's obscenity
or a fossil
is it because they hate seeing blood
think they are noble for taking
quick little showers
and using silicone at the farmer's market
I have never seen someone forgive themselves
as elaborately as the wealthy
everyone who paid for their wellness
is infecting the rest of us
yes I am sick sick sick
and want to sterilize all the ruinous overseers
though it is not like me to dream so much
I have managed to hoard something
that cannot be replicated
it will die when I die
let no one say we didn't try
to let a different kind of life bloom
and let no one say we didn't touch
what was there from the beginning

ariana's theme

I want to be authentic
w everyone like a child

becoming a person was easy

my mother was not involved
she was tiny pieces of herself
inside her mouthy cave
I was twitching from the wholeness
I heaved one great fart
after another after another
my greatest loves did not survive
tiny babies that never knew anything else
but their baby lives
I wanted to be babied too
I gave up everything to be babied
I told the love of my life
to baby me but he fell short
what if I was never born . . .
would you still want me?
if a person is happy five times or more
then that is a good life
I said that is a good life
there's no point in resisting
it's too late anyway—
we will figure out the rest from here

don't you get it

no one wants to see you
so in love
with who you have become

seppuku

because Dad forgot
the good cereal
I chose to seppuku
in the morning
I seppuku
to avoid washing my face
in the afternoon
I seppuku
to avoid conversation
I seppukued before bed
to feel stuff
I felt so much stuff
I had to seppuku
I felt so good
seppukuing!
to slay all stereotypes
I seppukued in front of racists
who were like, "OH MY GOD
THIS CHICK!"
and my dead seppukued body
was like, "uh huh!"
I died for racism
I died for white supremacy

I died for yellow peril
I seppukued three times
and each time
was more amazing than the last!
I actually want to seppuku
an entire country
and encourage the galaxy
to self-seppuku
to prove the necessity of repetition
that we must keep saying
SEPPUKU
and keep
SEPPUKUING
if we are to survive
if we are to be the animals
we were before we were
these exact beings
WE ARE NOW
and will always be

little tea party at home

every day I feel like telling my mom
how much
her lil cunt means to me
you're cute
I would say
if there was time
for anything at all
but there's no time
there's no today
or yesterday
yesterday's today
was not as sweet
as the cunty faces waving hello
we wave together
our two hands are one
teeny tiny funnel
we vomit
the darkest sperm possible
of all the places
anyone has ever fucked anyone
this is sooo the best
this chair
where my mom knitted

my first sweater
my first hat
my first scarf
my first gear
and ya germy splooge is not
that bad
and anyway
it's all worth it
to beam like catullus beamed
he knew my mom as well
as me
I love her
I love her
I love her
if I could cut up her lil cunt
and offer it to the dying—
like those
who have never known
the grace I have known—
I would do it immediately
before I lose my nerve
before I am overcome
with this need
to spend my days
sleeping at her feet
at the edge of her openings
lil dreams for lil things
for a second
I'd rather not live

I'd rather not know
like every dream
I ever wanted to have
& just about impossible
to remember
what it was
I said I would do

uncle boo

my boo gave me a yeast infection
iw as like ooo boooooooooooooooooooooooooo
ooooo
ooooo
ooooo
ooooo
ooooo
ooooo
i was like i'm gonna make you din
and i did
using the garlic
in my yogurt twat
we ate naan
and spread
& everyone i know
& will know
& want to know
was spread too
we re all spread out
happy as pictured
happy as described
happy
so happy

jenny's trying

why hide?

The Universal Energy Is About to Intervene in Your Life

I am pure emotion and you must pour me
this way the standards will instantly change
the nerves will stand on innards
me I am crammed full of beginnings
paid for respect and got none
all the unborn children
play in the same universe
they don't care they were never born
they don't care the stars were not created for them
they don't care they had panicked mothers
who could have changed
though now the world is perfectly populated
each time the future is altered
someone dies for no reason
this is how I became a ghoul
this is how I became a gaaaaaaaaaaaaaaaaah
this is how I became a guuuuuuuuuuuuuuuuuh
this is how I became a gaaaaaaaaaaaaaaaaaaaaaaaaaaaaaash
drinking the goo goo water
I decide that no one lives for anyone
I will live for me

I will die thanks to unconditional love
I want to ask my mother why she loved me
and for her to ask her mother why she loved her
and for her mother to ask her mother why she loved her
there are too many centuries of mothers loving their mothers
I will be the first to love myself more than I love my mother
I said *if I live to 99 I am gonna eat mercury*
but then I turned 9 and couldn't wait
and then this mercury eater lived another year
and another year
bloated with mercury
my future children swam like fish
I had the doctor sew me up
so food had to enter
the same way it came out
I lived like this for centuries
they said I could go on and I said
do I look like I would stop
and they said stop
and I said WHAT
and they said stop
and I said WAIT
is this really all there is?
I didn't want to believe it
but what else did I have
What else is there for us?
Those of us who cannot breathe
Those of us who cannot birth anything
We want to mean something to the world

We want to be told: stay
you are needed
and we are needed
someone needs us
They called for us to live this way and so I did and so I did
and so I did.

castles in the air for the very very

despite not having anything
resembling a core
or a life worth rescuing
they refuse to die
will they continue to surf
the drying seas?
will they motor past
the dead and the dying
to fuck whoever complies?
the purity of relationship anarchy
experienced only by the descendants
of murderers
all islands that still have land coverage
cryptopaid for
a nice addition to a v diverse portfolio
of stolen land
it's not enough for the greedy
to turn every travel destination
into a cultural plantation
for their freaking pleasure
they gotta build multiple properties
on the one meridian line
that can still survive the radius of fallout

every establishment with good coffee
& pesticide free vegetables
converts into another eviction for the poor
it is actually erotic
to believe in the end of the world
is it only catastrophe that gets you going?
would you still be hard if you knew
you couldn't survive this?
not everyone wants to live
and not everyone wants to die en masse
why are my people required
to recycle your trash
when did we agree to be on the dumping end
of your no-waste life
just being allowed to live is maybe a waste
& it won't be long before someone adds up
the energy it costs to keep a life like yours
meaningful in the way you've come to expect

yeast

i got a lot out of this
the more i got
the less there was
there was so much more
that i became significant
for the first time i was very
very and the constant
significance got to me
there is no rejecting
the infinite world
you know
and i know
the fumey whiff of love
was very very significant
i don't even wanna occupy
this already occupied space
anyway
we all cram in there
and love it
we love it here
we really love it here

You are the poorest person here

when I was born I was born
a victim
when you were born you were born
a hero
just kidding
you were anything you wanted to be
remember that you are supposed to
barf on me
& I am supposed to barf
on myself!

Go ahead
& say that I have not planned for my future
let's hear you say that
your degree in sociology
is as important as being an unborn baby
the day we dropped the atom bomb
you cloud
& the mushroom tip of your dick
is just disgusting!

I don't give if the third world makes hygiene
difficult
"I said I don't give if the third world
puts you at a disadvantage
I didn't choose to be born where I was born
& if your baby was not born
the day yr flower dress
got burned onto yr back
that's like
not my fault!"

Okay
so is it my fault
that I want to leave this poetry reading
so I can go look at the electrical fire
& applaud for the firemen
who we think are great
because they are not poets
but one of them says something
he's like, burhgh, and we ask for more!

my sword

I had little thoughts
so time could have more
it's not what we wished
but we have it now
I don't want to keep living
nor do I want to stop
the dead don't wanna be researched
the past isn't suitable for martyrdom
but there it was
all trusted and crammed into a citation
I swore in goo goo putong hua
and wrote in doo doo english
run my little friends
run from these maniacs
who keep telling us:
get over it
we're over it!
the centuries of tomorrow
already happened
we live in the best world possible
and anyone who says otherwise
shall die by my sword

My baby first birthday

my mom was a baby too
and inside her was a teenier baby
if not for that baby
I would still be
essentially an idea
I walk around with fists pulled up to my sides
when someone who has wronged me walks by
I hit the air
breezing past the goo goo
with my baby fists
my goo goo oozes goo
my cunt hurts
being disease free is a breeze
my mom's choco coco
gets inside of me and says, "goo!"
I feel close to her
we stay up late and scoop out goo
from one another's brilliant snatches
diurnal creatures can fuck off
we are quite happy this way

ariana's theme (reprise)

I am authentic w everyone
like a child

Natural

I don't know anyone
with the eyes I have
soft boundaries
slow aging
the medicine isn't working
I still have pain on my sides
nodes that no longer light up
switching between why and how
I become someone's mother
& give up the language
I was born into
this is okay
so you say
so you say
so say it then

ymca

y don't u know anyone like me
was it because you grew up in white working class
boston or bc you nibble little cubes of consommé
i was a bully before i was ever named
so everywhere there is a tiny border that did not
take into account who was there first
i'm talking about the land and no more spirituality
gained by travel funds and a house in your father's name
em is the place where you like it in your face
i found girl power as alienating as it was
apparent tho who knows? it is easier
to say what u know after some support
easier to say u are worse off than to die quietly
cee u have gained imagination mostly thru women
but i've never noticed u too shy to sign checks
or how come you started advocating for anonymity
at precisely the moment u were no longer relevant?
actually i take it all back
yr family was not facing extinction
tho fine it was like the thought was no longer
unthinkable so i do relate to the panic and the planning
an honest lifetime without pain is the dream
but no one lives as they sleep no one outlives

their own purity which is why diane di prima trends
online which is why ok ya i did take note
of the sample sentence on urban dictionary
antifa looks at black man with white straight laces
"are you a nazi?"
i for one don't know what's out there
how r all of u finding each other
why doesn't anyone fight in front of me
i can't defend it but i really don't wanna lose my teeth
i like my face mostly the way it is
i wouldn't like to give up my shiny hair
that isn't to say i should have anything at all
or like there's the enemy we imagine fighting
and the enemy who truly wants to nuke us
either way my instincts are nowhere close
to liberation which is why i care most
about my family in queens and my other fam
in the old country this is how it is if someone
threatens yr clan u show up unless u think u can get away
with meals as usual fucking before sleeping
a level of vanity that straddles beauty as terror
arms for hostages and another word
for another word i refuse to say c'mon %%%%%
%%%%% and %%%% and %%%%%
and %%%% and %%%% and %%%%
%%%%%%%%%%%%%%%%%%%%%%%%%
no matter how cowardly i dip i won't forget
my father's first year in america
he stole chlorine from the ymca for laffs

accidentally stepped foot in church bc of a sign
FREE FOOD FOR THE WEARY
he didn't identify as hungry
but anyway he went
anyway his id was recorded
anyway i lost my birth certificate in transit
anyway i wrote it all down and expect
what is commonly referred to as
nothing
nothing
nothing
nothing
nothing
nothing
nothing

suddenly I'm so hungry

I eat the whole world
I eat my mom's mom
your mom complained
she was like
what about me
I was like
and what about me?
everyone's always like
what about me?
but srsly
what about me?
no one is sailing anywhere interesting
no one is going to have the good life
their moms promised them
grace was mostly dead
but people made it the subject of art anyway
who are these people
do I know any of you people

Ell

yo this born winner thinks she owns me
it has to do with the time someone called her
racist and she invoked her own helplessness
when your birthright gives you everything
except the right to be liked
I got pulled into the ring
I had the right kind of face
to be a very effective shield
I had the right kind of ideas
to waste time arguing with hurt people
who seek penance from the fit & the well
is there really a class of people
who have never been hurt?
is that why these fights last so long?
what's the point of telling someone
"I've been kicked when I was down too"
what's the point of being rich
if all you can remember
is the time you ended up hospitalized
I know which fights I won't win
still I say yes to every opportunity . . .
the rich get soooooo emotional
about their property

sometimes I think I'll keep pinging
from one owner to the next
all them promising *you're sooo amazing*
the minute I stop bowing in gratitude
I can expect eviction I can expect humiliation
I'm used to just about anything
I'll bathe in orange peels and eucalyptus
if my skin glows too much
they'll put me through another toilet
and the gurgle gurgle of tomorrow
is all I've ever looked forward to or known

"revision"

i'm sorry i got rid of yr poems
it's just ugly to have this much dust
everyone's allergic and no one is sweet
not me
i'm what the old country refers to as
t h e   d r e a m
actually i am
at a birthday party i eat cake first
at someone else's wedding i announce
t h e   p o l i c e   s t a t e   i s   o v e r
actually it is
no more talking
all vows matter and this one especially
bc it is about wanting to just live
in this body i don't want anyone to see
i will rot when i choose
who ever thought that could be a kind
of rallying cry

there is only world

there is only world
why did it get so quiet
has anyone waited for their own
execution gracefully
no I don't think
I will turn in my father
no I don't think I will go against
my mother
anyone who birthed me
was wrong
to expect gratitude
the white settlers born free
will die free
in Canada
they are just waiting
for the immigration website
to load again
me I am in jail
in my own bed I melted
the softness I found in love
the muscle I gained
through repeated abuse
long notes that quiver

I don't think the state will protect u
no survivor can live without a layer
the first is the unutterable—
did you ask to be born?
to think the very first moment
happened without you knowing
no more talking at breakfast
stay lost and stay humble
some people didn't ask to be saved
but in the end it is almost impossible
to say no to more life

jenny's trying (reprise)

now is not the time to hide

with my mother in nice

my lover grows distant
I lose body parts to please them
no time to really investigate
has this body pleased no one?
is it true I was lucky to be born
into this carapace?
I nurture it at school
earn straight A's
cannot fight at all with this thing
dangling between us
when some guy steps to me
I say: this isn't real
he says: prove it
I can prove to anyone
this part of me works best
when it has been violated
I apologize to my cock
with my former cunt
they are on cordial terms lately
someone tells me
because I post my mom's English
to my online profile
I must not like myself

because I talk about seppuku
and its cuteness
I must not like my family
or the family that killed my family
back in the old country
all of this too true
I put a scoop of vanilla on the very tippy tip
eat sprinkles off my own growth & feel
more accomplished than churchill
perhaps because rebelais has no way
of talking to ceéline; those mouthcrops
better bloom daisies for I'm going home
where the dinosaurs perished
where my grandfather was buried
we touch his body
we know his whole entire life
we see it as clearly as ever

goo goo water

on my baby first birthday I drank goo goo water
my parents ate Mongolian beef
I had chicken with broccoli
my little brother had nine more years
to be born
in those nine years he swam in egg drop soup & went
goo goo to the whales who were goo goo to the krill
who were goo goo to the sea urchins who were goo goo
to the goo that live underwater like me
like me they don't swim
like me they don't swallow semen
if semen gets in their mouth
they just goo goo it onto another sick fuck
which is not as sad as not being who you say you are
which is not as sad as not being who you want to be
which is not as sad as not being who you could be
which is not as sad as not being who you should have been
I should have been born with big fat cunt lips for lips
I should have been born with a skinny regular cunt for a cunt
had I been then my lil cunt could have given farewell speeches
at the end of great moments like this moment
when my mother said she was glad she gave birth to me
& I said I was too & she knelt down by my cunt lips
& kissed the very mouth that said what had to be said

SPRING

Everyone's girlfriend

I wanna be everyone's girlfriend
crawl like a dead bug before I die
be born without consent
consent to everything when no one
has asked me to be anything
to have anything at all
would be brilliant too
I want to be brilliant
like tiny worms that live
inside your head are brilliant
like your head was brilliant
when you told me to have
some reason to exist
and I do
for some reason
I am not myself
it wasn't that sad
when I was my own gift
when I didn't have thoughts of my own
when I admitted I was stupid
when I gave up on living admirably
when I patched the hole I fell into
and knew I would stay there forever
and I knew I would live this way

and I knew I would want to want more
and I knew I wanted to be buried with everyone
with the dead stars that lead you home
with the child I won't have
because I need to have a perfect cunt
and because you know me
we now bond over our perfect cunts
we now bond over our perfect tits
we now bond over our perfect mutations
we now bond over our perfect facials
the sperm you drank from my ruined body
knows boundaries but we are too perfect
to adhere to someone else's idea of perfection
each idea born from an idea that proves
existence was not what God intended
but we speak for everyone now
and all of Asia changes when I change
which is why the world you live in
can no longer be stable
can no longer want anything
I want to be or feel awful
I want to repent or show you
I am good and my saintly practice
has a home at last
and I am deserving
though it is true I cannot be the first one
to say so

it's spring

everyone's still so flippin ugly
my romance will lead itself
no one who wears flip flops
as their primary footwear
has ever given to the poor
- anyway -
redistribution of wealth
has gone the way of democracy
how many times have you carried on
a relationship with a corpse
we bow 3 times to the dead
and this guy has the nerve
to perform western psychology
on my shanghai family
well eff u cee kay kiss my broken
finger blade I don't feel like
making excuses today
did a soda company really
collude with the state
I'm on the five star of yesterday
if it doesn't fit inside a post
what is it even
you must have known you'd lose

your privacy the day you wanted
someone to compliment you
what does it take
for anyone to see anyone
if history is true
then you and I
are either rare or doomed
at your request
I actually do try to remove
myself from public life
"would that make you happy?"
but I know how this works
you'll want more of me to vanish
more and more and more
until all of us are gone
leaving you and your family money
and your buddies from harvard and yale
and yr polycube
suddenly my favorite line
grows sinister
"we shall have everything we want
and there'll be no more dying"
the always-sorry tremble
like the smallest creatures
waiting for the boot
waiting to die of natural causes
so you can finally have your paradise

screenshot for later

I fear the situation has been set up
for renewed intimacy
between two lonely people
who cannot fully give to or get from
the other what they want

It was a period when cunt was in the air

"I went at her slam-bag and shot it in her guts"
It felt goo to get that far
my mother was goo to me and I promised her
one day I would split up her cunt again
so blessed she would feel
to have birthed the same child twice
to be re-stitched and re-praised
a sensation like petting a mutt who appears
in the stony gutted scooped-out rictus
of your last brilliant dream!
clap your hands if you're sick of being you
clap your hands if you need more nice sploogee
on warm nights when you wish to swim well
& clap your hands if you think you have enough
holes if you ever wanted to shit from yr pits
if you can admit doing jumping jacks
gets you pumped
place de clichy is so bitching sweet
the lycée where I teach is so tooootally me
but still there's something
still I am unsettled
I feel I must have more
I feel I must feel more

I feel I must know more
I feel I must drink more
when other people are around
when the given prophet undoes his cremaster
I will be there with a warm compress
& melting candy on the tip of my tongue
saved from my baby first birthday
next year when I turn thirty
you promised me cumcakes!
you said you would enlist yr brothers
I said: don't deplete yourself for me
but really I'm not worried about that
if anything I'm worried you won't!
but still I look forward to tomorrow
& still I look forward to the next day
I guess I just want to smash a cumcake in my face
eat the frosting with my fingers
& enjoy the celebration
the suddenly formed procession
we walk from my childhood home
right back to my childhood home
and end up here
where I ask those of you who know me
to clap your hands if you came to see what would happen
clap your hands if you came because I asked you to

HAMMER

I kept dripping yesterday's goo
on my silver slippers
he said, "don't bother me
with yr micro problems
where yr from
what yr eyes look like
that's not my business—
find something deeper
or don't cry about it
as for me
I have always
and will always
be team USA"
he went around barking
odious sounds of joy
and waving little mini flags
in ribbony twirls
I won't kid myself—
I was never a Tonya
and I wasn't a Nancy
if I had to be mistaken for anyone
it would have been Michelle
who wasn't even born in China

who placed second after Tonya
who was bumped for the white girl
showdown
Nancy had a bashed knee
so she had to go
Tonya had never been loved
she also had to go
I guess everyone has wondered
at some point or another
WHY
WHY
WHY
WHY ME?
right now for example
I wonder how and WHY
some people's cruelty
can know no bounds
unmatched by all the love
I have ever known
as if the conscious study of tenderness
never meant anything to anyone
except those of us who never did get used to
never meaning anything to anyone
we who live in real live graveyards
& those of us not born
with the right to anything
found it totally inverted
we shall have nothing we want
and there'll be no more living

O! there was still a dream
in between all the miseries
from one puberty to the next
we complained when our women
moved on from being girls
still we were keen to watch the next group
thick ones recognized each other
not to say I was recognized
the truth is I'm not ashamed of my body
though it is true
I'm scared to love it publicly
the woman from Wuhan brought us pickled wormwood
juicy plums fermenting inside prickly pears
followed me into the bathroom
and stared at me staring at her staring at me
until finally she asked for my autograph
thinking I was her favorite figure skater
I scribbled, "with love, Michelle <3"
it was the only time I had been glad
to be mistaken for someone else
who had been mistaken for an other
she was sent to Lillehammer as an alternate
—for years I thought it was a *lil* hammer
in college I carried hammers in my bag
ready at a moment's notice
to smash the white supremacist police state . . .
I wasn't trying to be
someone who calls the cops
when their car gets broken into

and their stash stolen
guess anyone can be a druggie
anyone can be mistaken
in 1998 I drank just a little tiny bit of pee
it was my witchy phase
I was doing anything to get deported
the newspaper my father brought home
said, "American beats out Kwan"
how did two Chinese girls ever think
we would be someone?
in 2002 I was fucking performatively
on someone's private lawn
in my private university
there was the ugly low hanging moon
a big gash in a world I never wanted anything less
than big pulsing beatific love
"American outshines Kwan"
"she was the crybaby who didn't win the gold . . ."
I've never said that before
I'm not afraid to love someone
who doesn't see me
well if I am to be graceful like you said I was
if I am to be light as you say I am
if you are to ask me when my dreams end
as you've asked me
I will tell you what I saw:
that fluttering peplum
the girl mistaken for my twin
all the mistaken twins in the world

weaving through each other's dreams

little outshined trails that go drippy and gooey and ugly

swear we meant it when we said

"I feel fine" and anyway it was a woman's sport

before it was a girly pageant

when the reporter tried to get her to repeat herself

Nancy spoke like a woman

her noble blood was created by someone

whose father had her same nose

it went on and on and on until the last referent

dismissed the whole line of nobility

"WHY me? I can't think that viciously"

"hi America, hi Europe"

hi Asia too

as a young girl

I honestly wanted to be white trash

hi mom

hi dad

I waved like Nancy next to Mickey Mouse

bratty and over it

it was the first parade where I touched ice

that thin blade holding me

if I wobbled it was merely that I felt

we were under the most forgiving of all suns—

winter sun

blowing winter light

thru endless puberty—

a girlhood that never sours

it's so intoxicating to be unwell

y/n?

NO

once one of us does something
the other one immediately does it too
no
N-O
NO
there's no we
just you

THERE IS NOTHING TO SAY

There is nothing to say
There is nothing to say
there is nothing to say
there is nothing to say
there is nothing to say
there is nothing to say
there is nothing to say
there is nothing to say
there is nothing to say
there is nothing to say
there is nothing to say
there is nothing to say
I have something to say
there is nothing to say
there is nothing to say
there is nothing to say
there is nothing to say
there is nothing to say
there is nothing to say
there is nothing to say

there is nothing to say
there is nothing to say
there is nothing to say
there is nothing to say
there is nothing to say
there is nothing to say
there is nothing to say
there is nothing to say
there is nothing to say
there is nothing to say
there is nothing to say
there is nothing to say
there is nothing to say
there is nothing to say
there is nothing to say
there is nothing to say
there is nothing to say
there is nothing to say
there is nothing to say
there is nothing to say
there is nothing to say
I have no idea what to say

spring discourse

sorry i broke into yr   nogoo relationship   it's really
nice to be insignificant   guess i'm not gonna fly standby
on united anymore   guess i'm mad about the praxis of the
comfortable bragging about ma ke si   yes i'm sure he sucked
white dick   yes i heard u loud and clear   u can't be racist
because of who u fuck   ofc *i'm* the one fretting   he
finally gets "emotional labor"   was the education worth
it?   so indoctrinated i actually feel ashamed things are *equal*
between us   well get the fuck over it   no one likes u
more than me   and no one respects u less than u respect
yourself   this is all very apparent   v nice   v wild swans
long fingers wet teeth   get drunk for me then make yrself
wet   i said if u show me dry panties i'll leave u   i
still won't go on the record   u don't care what happens
to my family   when i speak 4 them   but i do i freaking do

I feel nothing but hatred hatred
hatred hatred

it turns you on
until you know me
come here I say
get to know me already

it brought you

to this very moment
despite all the pain
& "wasted time"

Don't

or if you do it then be
right and if you are right be
relentless like this was relentless
when you spoke to that bitch
she was just That Bitch
and you were A Good Guy
and that was the first time My Lips
wanted to be just lips
my entrenched feelings have a way
of making themselves known
to know me is to know my mother's bad English
the time I charmed you with not wanting
to not want to not take a shit
in my pants which were yours
the smell was also yours
you gave me the constipated figurine
I washed it like it was my own
and it was your face that gave me the finest idea
the idea of not having any more ideas
was good enough if it meant saving the idea
of you or the time you yanked metal
from your hand which does not leave me
even when my face is no longer a face

and my ideas no longer ideas
just the fine french doors you live inside
like I live inside this promise
like you live inside my dreams
the best ones where you did not yet exist
though I knew this fine universe
would create you eventually
and I would never stop thanking my mother
for creating me too

Is it possible for me to become the person you love the most in your life

in this other world
children sit on bended knee
the elderly have great bodies
the young know exactly what to say
the streets flood with big fat tears
no one is afraid of pain
death finally inconsequential
I think of how lovely it would be
to possess buttholes
capable of prehensile movement
to hold on is a curse and a gift
I want to live
where the dead are
never carried
so obviously
a thing of the past
what dignity it is to become more
everything that has ever gone wrong
converted into a thin bubble
ya I acknowledged I was cruel
ya I know how I seem from the outside

all there ever was was a feeling
that can never be recreated by anyone
but the feeler
who has long since stopped

tanaïs's theme

how many generations of women
are we descended from
who never chose themselves

I had a lot to say

miss wiener told me to say it
miss weil told me to say it
miss ass-to-no told me to say it
I said it and said it and said it
it was all of france
and europe
and the part of russia
where everyone lives
that is still europe
miss no-no said there are people
who live in the part of russia
that is *technically* asia
whaaaaaaaaaaaa?
we use the internet to memorize
really lovely images
which proves beauty
does not obliterate pity
I have the most pity of anyone
more than the moon has pity
for its baby moon
who has pity for its baby brother
who back on earth
is a dot we draw on our eyelids

so every time we blink
we feel too large to exist
and it is that largeness
that big big moon
wailing big big ideas
on her baby first birthday
when her mother carried her to us
like it was a holiday
the first day on earth
every living creature already
sinners not yet been told
all this misery
all this shiny stuff
all of it
all of it we say
is possible
all of it you say
we have
it is possible
it is possible
this prayer makes it
possible & ours
forever

why would you ever be friends with her?

you must be desperate
or one of those people
who actually look forward
to more segregation
honestly that's everyone *****
everyone under the spell of *****
supremacy only gets hard if power's present
you're one of them aren't you
you're hot for tax evasion
your grandaddy's an oil baron
yet somehow you're solidly middle class
and still collect five dollars from everyone
when you pull into an hourly lot
euphemism is the only erotics
you've been known to practice
do you dry up and go limp
when someone calls for accountability
you've never seen yourself
paired up with someone like me
essentially a poor person with taste
no one said so but I can tell
my family is why everyone else moved away
I've always wondered but never asked

is your charisma a marriage
between being born lucky and finding a way
to still be damaged?
the endless hours of nobility
and lack of struggle
must really rot the mind
your dimpled ass doesn't make me cry
your bad acne doesn't warrant a solo show
what can I even say
the worst day of your life
looks exactly like one of my best
the time my father brought home carvel ice cream
and the whole fam ate it with our lil wiggling toes
can you even imagine
the ppl you haven't really gotten to know
so cute and geniusy

Groupon

I'm supposed to want
a facial
but um
what they don't get
is I can get one
at no charge
not to mention
I've never stopped
to think
what do I want
what in this world
is free

Fidget

"I feel too sad to live"
that's what everyone keeps saying
I want to meet someone
who knows how to live
is this person on the internet
is this person on pinterest
I tell my mom I am happy
and life is good
but busy
I tell her I don't need to have a family
I can go to bed earlier if I need to
I would like it if she heated up porridge in the morning
there is so much to tell so many people
at so many different times in my life
I feel like I am drunk again
though not sloppy
what if I am not a very good person
there it is again—
needing answers—
I keep thinking what if this had happened
what if that had happened
what if I had done this at that time
what if everything was different

what if people could stop telling me to stop
wondering about what could have been
because maybe all of this is important
maybe I cannot be anything else right now
but I still want
to be anything
I still want to go back into the past
and change how everything was
and change myself back then
so I wouldn't have to change as much now
I wake up early
I wake up screaming
these clothes have no future
I think I see someone I used to know
on the street
I cannot move and I wish
I were dead
I honestly wish I were dead
I pretend to be my own friend
and I say to me—as my friend—
"if you really wanted to be dead . . .
I'm just saying . . ."
there are a lot of good experiences to be had
but not right now
I could be writing really well
but not right now
right now I can't do anything
I want to be free and alone
not talking about cunts

and everyone who wants to control one
I don't want to drive a bus full of cunts
I don't want to apply for insurance in case one of these cunts dies
I don't want to write "cunt death" below the dotted line
it's not like I'm not aware
no one thinks I should drive
not even if my cunt is steering
you admit that kinda intrigues you
I like it so much
when you are intrigued
but I can't do that right now
I can't have anything at all
I'm too far away and too tired
I told you I would do it later
I told you I would do it if I could
I told you I wanted to be a lone for long as

jenny's trying / victoria's theme

but i'm not an easy woman
and why would you want to be?

Someone

in the summers I would become someone
I wouldn't have to try very hard
it would just happen
the tall grass and the short hairs
I wanted my skin to touch the others
ghosts came in
which is to say memories
why do seaside vacations remain forever
the dress with the buttons and the wet bottoms
how they carried me through the bluffs
and set me down next to an old mermaid
she was uglier than I had come to expect
it was terrifying to think I would get old
and all glamorous things would have to be diagnosed
I guess it was about eroticizing the American dream
wet hot sweaty summer and the freedom to show off
why did I have to be so lonely and easily disappointed
why did it have to mean everything
why did I cry intermittently and always in private
whyyyyyyyyyyyyyyyyyyyy was I ever born

remember / it brought you (reprise)

it's not even your fault
that you displaced self-love
it all brought you
to this very moment
despite all the pain
& "wasted time"

Aegean

for my whole entire life
had been spent
with no thought of you
imagine the horror
a world enforced by thought alone
my life in pick-uppable parts
dribbling dirty streaks
down the naturally creamier parts
in in in in in in in in in in in in in
I said in-voluntarily
it was like a lifetime of p in v
crammed into just a look across a long room
I have not looked that long or that far
since I swam thru the other side
in my old flesh
now in in in in in in my new
new new mew mew I couldn't even
quit the leafy purring
if I held back with all hands
curling thru all toes
my hairs would still stand on end
I would still blink wildly at dead moons
the endless crinkling of their winters

a signal I had been hearing
even before I was alive
and now my second love
carries me across seasons
makes me as soft as when I was an idea
and all that boredom
fluffy and worth it
leetle tip of your finger
touching all the gooey parts
my secret sorrow
& my secret joy
offered up without limit
offered up without dying
all this life to be spared
to have been here all along
shyly waiting to go on or go on

SUMMER

your pubes are everywhere

your pubes are everywhere
when I sleep
they cover me like my mother's blankets
cover me
when I eat
they stay in the gaps between my teeth
and I savor them
like I savor dark meat
like I savor endless moments
like I savor the end of eternity
like I savor the meaty bits
the bush from whence we were conceived
lil animals who arrive sans pubes
lil beasts who cannot wait to trim the pubes
they do not yet have
lil pubes that cannot wait to live their dead life
I cannot wait to be reborn a pube
sprouting from your perfect hairless asshole
the rosebud that was invaded
by a single pube
me who loves you
who loves your pubes
as much or a little less than I love you

I mean as much or a little more than you
I meant to tell you
your pubes are everywhere
your pubes must live where I live
your pubes must know as much as I know
your pubes must feel sad when I feel sad
your pubes must spread and multiply
when the world is no more
when you are no more
when I am no more
when it's a matter of life or death
that your pubes go on
and I won't be there to appreciate
the art left behind by the dead
whatever it was they wanted to communicate
to the next world
is left to the hands of those
appointed to decipher the past
I am not one of those
I am not going to decipher anything
I just want to float on the dried up seas
I just want to floss my teeth
I just want to attach curlies to my eyes
and bat an eyeful of pubes
at the next beautiful man I see

Great

your daddy won't log off; he lives
to make women carry eyelashes in their tummies
all that time my twat was suspended in fluid
must have really made me gummy and flexible
it is absolutely true some people go to their graves
without coming to terms with the harm they've caused
is there anyone who doesn't have at least some figure
in mind standing in for what they are owed?
I did not mark the notabilia of your mother's house
so ornate and delirious with collecting
as a person often mistaken for an object
I did not think to behave with human dignity
instead I crawled sluggishly
like I had been salted in broad daylight
slabs of my skin pounded into gold
sprinkled across your antique wallpaper
should anything happen you can take to your legacy
publications and I will go online again
I know how much you disagree with my value
all that interest is just puffery until it threatens
your family line; don't think I don't realize
who ancestry.com has been scamming
when I speak in the first person it's memoir

& when you do it's a commencement speech
well you can't uninvite me to that FB group
"Harvard memes for h*rny b*urg*ois teens"
then lecture my people on the artlessness of confession
we laugh at you behind yr back you know
though it doesn't affect your balances
you can barely keep up with the acronyms
still you are paid for photographing salad
& I waste hours screenshotting receipts
no wonder my family turned violent
no wonder they didn't believe me
when I announced I would tend to roses
live a quiet life mostly inside except to water
go home go home go home go home go home
I heard the song and I know the law
sure I won't last long
& my legacy is uncertain
death or history will dispose of me perfectly
yr on the wrong side of history
types the daughter of a colonizer
who invites me to dinner after
I get published in her daddy's paper
I accept graciously then
go straight into hiding

brittani's theme

call them
text them
who cares

dumb theory

candy mottled whores or layered
clinker donkey
the stench of a heroine's creamed fats
over cream by introducing cream
that doth cream and sponge cream
amid cream to finish cream I go
cream
I'll take to deserve cream
"no, indeed"
"to finish the scenic route"
I cream as much as I care
to cream okay
there I go
fluffy sugar creamed fats
over cream
techniques of the creamed
I like to see cream
I like intrigue
the scenic route
the Pacific object
the industrial heroine
the volume of "cream"
to "creamed" is the volume

of cream philosophy introducing
the charm of cream
the charm of other origins
the charm of "under creaming"
the charm of a destination
the heroine's ceremony
an object to be admired
to deserve a heroine
to deserve a ceremony
to deserve
indeed, to deserve as much
indeed, to demand as much!

I know others before me have been this way

who isn't listening in this holding cell
was there even enough sadness
to make sense
someone who is not my hero
is singing just to be praised
I let it happen
my feet don't move correctly anymore
the stairs give me starry eyes
I would live even better than this
but no one will give me a chance

I'm a 30 year old White non racist male, with some of my closest friends being Black. With that being said

your grey t shirt bothers me

your green mules bother me

your white linen pants bother me

your heidi braids bother me

your good face which would make an equally good leg bothers me

your pierced ears and the crusty blood stain of not wearing 14 karat
    gold bothers me

your very good posture bothers me

your knowing what to say in difficult situations bothers me

your teeny tiny voice that makes mothers out of sisters bothers me

that I want to mother you very well is something

is it though

is it that your swept untiled floor bothers me?

your folding chairs neatly lined in ten rows by ten rows by ten rows by
ten rows bother me

your naked ambition so fleshy and dead and nutty bothers me

your mini bangs bother me

your plastic plants smelling like plastic flowers smelling like plastic
oranges smelling like dead hair smelling like plastic leaves
smelling like late spring when it no longer enables me to feel so
much bothers me

could you tap your freaking fingers on my freaking leg some more

when someone says *goo*, I perk up! and listen!

the passing thru of my baby dreams in print

unless the Vietnamese dispute yellow rain journalists won't get involved

unless a Harvard scientist says so no one has said it

I know a Harvard scientist

he farted in the pitch dark and we smelled it for days

his best joke is the one about the stuff around a pussy

he carries his own in a shopping bag

he once crossed the street for a hoodie

"so much piping" I said

"so much piping" I said

"so much piping" I said

these holding places

these great moments

what if it's all placeholders what if they do not name the thing itself

what if anyone can help it

and still

I cannot help it

your champion shoes bother me

your double eyelid from birth bothers me

your diatribe against surgery bothers me

your hatred of fake tits bothers me

your hatred of real tits bothers me

your fingernails all filed down and elegant bother me

your warbly bird voice that will one day carry me to the Baltic Sea if
    I wanted to be carried if I wanted to see the Baltic Sea if I wanted
    to be capable of pity the sorrow of being born lucky if I wanted
    to fart well on the illuminated texts of my oppressors if I wanted
    to have European distinctions if I wanted to live that deeply if I
    wanted to be around good breath if I am carried to the Baltic Sea
    if I finally bathe in the Baltic Sea if I finally see the Baltic Sea
    and you call out to me in yr trillsong and I don't have it in me to
    let it be carried out by the sea winds and I suddenly remember
    how tenderly your voice bothers me

the good air bothers me

the ring finger so ordered and so adventurous bothers me

Baudelaire struck dead by a little old lady!

like so what

like whatever

anyway like

just die

at the appropriate moment

my fingernails collapse so dead and so bright

why should anyone name what might be true

I got two names and was born in one place

I don't bother with so much

as things happen I decide

okay I can

or okay I can not

I will go for forty five minutes

in 10 years my heroes won't have time for me
in 5 years her translator will want to write his own shit
in 1 year I will be exactly the same
dropping loose pubes on the gorgeous rooftops
I keep seeing everywhere
the Baltic states are calling to me
the effluvia of tomorrow too sweet and too plaintive
to ignore
the lyric I speaks for itself
I have this feeling like time is very soft and lovely
slow down sisters!
let me hear you!
Let me!
Let meeee!
Let meeeeeeeeeeeee!
sometimes I don't understand why
you didn't just stop
I feel like a total imperialist
not wanting to sit thru something
in another language
after all
my own people
rode horses over the mountain and fell

tits-first into the river
into the cup of trembling
how overfull and still it was
truly wonderful to piss a streaking comet
and watch everyone down there go:
O! This is once in a lifetime isn't it?

from the dead dark into the green

tonight I will eat
cold chicken
live like an old queen
perspiring with mystery
flaunting my old stunner ways
and my frequent sightings
do I live on a cloud yet
there is too much goo
while waiting for a kava
at Teacher's house
I leak goo on my lita
while waiting for the group
I notice my goo trail
going everywhere I go
into the recommended museums
eating at the recommended restaurants
feeling very appropriately
at every single moment
at every single opportunity
to feel something
I do
I truly do
I feel so much that I goo

on my own leg
on the desk where my notebook
is open to a new page
there is no time to clear the mess
to take notes and follow instruction
friends, my computer has been hacked
"another lie"
I watched porn and vomited chicken
last year's queen told me
how boring life really can be
I know everything there is to know
and I'm not even curious
about the truth
some goat ate right off my hand
and I would flippin love it
if I could

We must rapidly begin

the western arrogance of feelings
my ancestors had ancestors too
they wore sheep faces and renamed the orient
"the orient"
but in their own language
is there anything to be said
about my own language
rounding the corners of l's I say
I love you and I rub you
the tradition of going somewhere
the tradition of saving someone
real heroes who won't wait
for monuments
for plaques carved from ancient stone
it's not just heroes who admit
to oneiric ways of resolving the past
I boo him so he knows my limits
at least I have some
the tradition of getting someone hard
just by saying
"I've been thinking about this all day"
is really something else
I had to be taught to shift

from a thing-oriented society
to a person-oriented society
but yr thing is like the only thing
I have that many feelings about
my ancestor's thingie
stayed solid thru the evening
and for once it feels right to say
it is as if my entire life up until then
had been in service of everyone else's dreams
there is something about speaking
when the other person does not know
when I am known finally
you will bend one knee so gently
the bees will have flowers of their own
their princely ballads will remind us
of who we so valiantly fantasized about saving
I speak now as a child of God:
let me have my moment
I recline and recline and recline
into the bright nothing I speak wastefully
into the bright nothing I go
. . . will you come with me?
we aren't meant to do it alone

It is finally midsummer

butterflies with translucent orange wings
make kissy faces at my half liquid turd
the only reason I shat in the grass
is because I feel combative and entitled
I would seek romance at every turn
but I'm too entitled
I know these two notorious hags
who give the greatest blowjobs
their cowabuuuuungie promises
make me shit blood so sharp
I cut lesions thru the pissed-on flowerbeds
the jungle floor sings so sweetly
the animal kingdom grows greener and greener
"at least ten percent goes to a charity
that endeavors to put an end
to the funding of more charities"
my gawd
someone listen to someone and make a decision
about anything already
some hags tell their own story
& I wish a different type of person
could be moved by what moves me
I don't want to admit what I see

in the million refracting weird little cries
actually gives me hope
my errant bloodturd finally
on its way
I feel free & bad
not watching the videos
my mom sends me from wenxuecity
I feel bad when I see she's liked
her own facebook status
free when I see her looking beautiful
under the cold shadowless light of midday
& I know there is a witness for everything
a type of submerged expectation that spoils
don't tell me yr gash drips like mine
don't tell me it could have been your son
don't tell me you aren't sleeping well at night
don't tell me you felt the weight of hopelessness like a millstone
    dragging holes thru the floorboards
don't tell me it was senseless
don't let your sadness come naturally
don't cry when I'm not ready to yet
don't make me think you know exactly what I know
that if it happens to one of us it happens to all of us
you cannot be one of us
I am not even one of us
& if I expected someone here to understand
then I'm just as stupid as I th-thought I was

the morning of yesterday's yesterday
is for once soft

my grandfather's afterlife
a locker room
full of the ashes of martyrs
the gooey dead walk soft
and sweet on my two capable feet
they go where I go
they pet me when I am the most alone
they tell me I can
I- I- I absolutely can

I have to

treat myself right
& you have to treat me right too
& still manage to treat yourself right

I would have no pubes if I were truly in love

this I know
this I am sure of
the only non-white person at the poetry reading
was totally related to me
I don't call anything a dream
your primeval stink really gets me
I think fucking is p in v but later
my mom tells me there's more
is p pussy and v vagina, I say
you must try everything, she says
I say it too always striving
to be someone's mirror
everyone tells me I am my mother's mother
both of us were born with curly pubes
that straightened out late in life
she tells me about a Chinese academic
and I'm like, I'm a Chinese academic!
and she's like, yeeeah
but not like him
so yeeeeeeeeeeeeeeaaaaaaaah
I'm not like him

I don't have anything to say
I don't have very many ideas
after falling in love I smell medicinal shit
everywhere
trying to locate the source
I trace it to the inside of my bedroom walls
"if you never marry and stay in New York
no one will ever see the lovely paintings
from your childhood that hang on your walls"
yah mom, I know that
is that what you want, she inquires
I know the answer
I know my answer
I know the answer
still I don't think I have enough
still I don't think I think enough
at home I make Minnie Mouse dive into my muff
and I swear to god she's the only one
who gets me: "you, my dear Minnie
are my best and only friend
no one else in this whole world understands"
at the library I swear to god
I shit myself standing up
reading *Sweet Valley High*
squeezing my cheeks with determination
when Bruce Patman "grazes" Elizabeth's breast
later I swear to god I wrote "graces" her breast in my diary
and I am so excited by this first evidence of poetic greatness
that I wipe my big sloppy cunt lips on my diary

so I can frame it and get it shown
in the next Whitney Biennial
I know lots of white guys
who have done this
who have rejected their family wealth
framed their own cum
splattered against the front page of yesterday's newspaper
I have been offered day-old semen
in a champagne glass that came with the discounted Moet
my mom bought from Costco
it is important to get a good deal on cum-vessels
tomorrow I think I shall shop in bulk for flour and sugar
so that I can bake cum cakes
for my own true love
how good I am
how saintly my practice becomes
how generous I naturally can be
it's everyone's party
it's everyone's right
"just because it offends u doesn't mean
u you should make everyone else feel like shit"
just because most days I feel like doo doo
doesn't mean you shouldn't say sorry
every once in a while
every once in a while
my mom is all like, say sorry
and I'm all like, say sorry
and she's all like, say sorry without the say
and I'm all like, say sorry without the say!

I bet if she could
she'd stuff me right back up her lil cunt
and we would fulfill each other
in ways we cannot dream of now
it is not so doo doo to be admired
when someone says:
I dream of your rice paper skin
and those almond milk eyes
and your water lily breath
gets my American hamburger
so completely solid
I am like, yah I know
you think I don't see myself the way you see me?
but I'm not gonna make this about me
I'm not gonna eat Keats's eye after all and use it
to see who will read me when I'm dead
to see who will write about the women in the fire
after the rest of New York's landfill floats away
I swear I am related to every single person
who has ever suffered
not that this is about me
or my suffering
or how I am at the center of all this
how no one has ever had it
the way I have had it
people who know me ask:
how does it feel that the most tragic thing about you
is something the average person cannot ever see?
it feels secretive, I shall say at the next party

it feels wonderful, I shall say at the next dinner
it feels tremendous, I shall say at the next wine and cheese
I feel everything, I shall say to the one person
who has suffered nearly as much as me
we are both so lucky, I shall say
we have both lived so much, I will say
don't you think so? I find myself saying
don't you feel it to be true?

shamepuff

I don't have too many feelings
anymore than the first
finicky morning of morning
final moments
when I am mourning the I who you said
was very nice & sometimes
I am tender
I can be sweet too
the cars zip in and out and in and out
I make a move to be someone
and then cannot
it feels very honest to want
to be someone's wife
if my hubby would only say
her cunt is the tastiest of them all
I would ask him to repeat it
but he holds me down and tells me
you don't get to have everything
in all of this is I is I is I is I is I
need to go to the DMV
I am going to go to the DMV
I wear a dress so short
my pussy hangs out like

with the guys
in all of this is my pussy
is my pussy is my pussy is my pussy
waiting in line at the DMV
vibrating with boredom so deep
I end up goo gooing
all over my best friends
some of them are still here
they write me on my baby first birthday
my poonie pony apologizes to your spooky sploogieee
it's okay
I don't need health insurance
to see a doctor
my mother will live as long as I live
I will love my family forever
when my best friends get married
and start families
I will play along and make my feelings
be nice to my other feelings
I said it once and I'll say it again
my feelings have feelings
my dreams have dreams
they know what is in store for me
they see what I cannot see
leave me speechless
& I don't think I could change
not even if I wanted to
not even if I knew

communication ≠ connection

what if there was something softer?
"no one is smarter than themselves"
I don't feel like getting super quotable
it's not a vibe if it's uncompensated
not everyone can be sloppy and get away with it
legacy girls for example look best undone
not me or my mother or my cousins or my aunties
it's too easy for us to look poor
the wrong kind of interesting
is worth at least noting
at least I don't worry about a bullet thru my brain
at least when I talk I'm only silencing myself
something that looks bad in photos and tastes good in real life
a book that has to be held sideways
that's how my ancestors did it
read up to down right to left
their descendants avoid going too far south
they don't get how they're lumped in
I guess it's time to accept blame
I hid my origins to fit into that lit party
where the editors walked around erect
for 19th century French décor
"I'm afraid we don't publish much memoir"

will anyone stand up and point out
how melodramatic and revealing it is
when men efface themselves
I could say I know everything about
why he chose to go into war journalism
. . . starting with his four hour sunburn . . .
I like it when white people have the faces
they deserve
they called for destruction & largely got it
I mean who am I kidding
we were extinct so long ago
all you're seeing now
is a dream that lives
only as long as the dreamer

worried

I'll revert back to how I was

a monster

I didn't know better

like most of my brothers
you grew up watching everything
expecting anything
well
me too
but honestly
I'm more fascinating
and less studied
and so many men have told my story
it sounds copied when I tell it
it seems trite to be moved by it
I don't mind sucking
my menstrual blood
a gesture to ease you
into eating your own cum
some men snowball
without knowing
some women become high ranking
without trying
all these differences are important
up to a point
I guess
I thought you were gay

after I jerked you off
for the camera
on the bed
where it was soft
yes I hovered over you like a seraphim
yes I looked down on you and saw what I saw
too lazy to be anything but prone
I accidentally jerked a load
onto your face
"O God!
It's in my eye!"
but you love facials
in fact you've always insisted on them
you walk around like a child of god
you won't have what I have
if you aren't gay then what are you
just another man
without imagination
just another boy
who never noticed
the entire family
sitting around at dinner
waiting to see
what part of the chicken
he would eat first
so we would know to abstain
from chewing on the stringy neck
your greatest feature
is you never have to ask

but I look at your watery eyes
and I feel so pleased
a face full of cum . . .
I pull down your lip so it dribbles in
I feel like cloning you to give you a full bukkake
I feel like cloning you to make you a lucky pierre
I feel like cloning you so you may watch yourself eat
that greedy gurgly mouth
I'm sure
if you could see yourself
you would turn away too

which is why I am telling you about this now

it won't go wasted on me
pink morning came on time
the worst haters mostly out of my life
still we have fun
haven't I looked out enough windows
haven't I lived on three continents
still my people call for me
this was not the journey they were forced to take
my thing was a pleasure thing
had to look up blue moon to enjoy it
I wasn't born in the same country
your childhood wasn't mine
your ghostly ache was felt in my bed
when another poet served opium cocktails
I was instantly humiliated
he heard me from the other room
we were having the same dream
someone finally came to take me away

A troll

I know this one girl knows
plenty of black and brown ppl
I see them pop up on her feed
on her trips to West Africa
and to India and Nepal
she must write her own captions
he was the kindest bellhop
his love for life inspires me
she so loves
the wretched
she's in line for sainthood
wants blamelessness above all
it's not like you don't have
your own form of misery
it's not like you haven't
gone thru some real shit
I know you have lived
I know you have felt loss
I know you have known a kind of hunger
which honestly
could have killed you
and you survived
just like them

when it comes to ppl who own land
they always wanna be at the level
of ppl who don't
without giving up anything
the only cure for the leisure class
& their fetish for self-destruction
is subaltern tourism
on paper you claim hardship
as if hoarding knowledge
has no monetary value
& I can't even say shit to you
because apparently
you are beyond generous
"if I'm such a monster
then why did I tip him a full
twenty dollars every morning?
o right because only monsters
give 200% tips"
I let you rant bc
I'm going to die soon anyway
I'll die hearing this
& I'll die holding it in
& anyway no one feels more
for anyone else
than they do themselves
all our pain
all our kindness
all going in the same direction
the instinct to protect family

& create it
is so ugly
why does anyone praise it
a year later I see her
posting pictures of a slain black boy
I comment from a burner acct
"a friend of yours?"
& the next thing I know
I'm blocked
I guess all along
I was nothing
but a troll

haha hey

sorry wait
I don't really
understand
the question
bounding
across the dark
dead to the green
green
you might
run away
screaming
at the site
of me
yr loved thing
crapping on a fence
I clap
for anything
the dark dead
and the light
behind
dad's ears
a gated park
circled boundaries

record
neediness
we are alive
though still
I don't know
am I evil??
am I????
am I
a good person
or not
a bunch of people
staring at one
very obvious
O WOW
thing
I'm staring too
openly
at you
the frame
is shaking
on a loved thing
his ass is white
and wild

Baby's first birthday

In Paris, I am Baby
my hair grows and grows and grows—

beigy people in white clothes talking about purity
& the tanning industrial complex

"you speak perfect English, there's no accent at all"

to be so Baby you have to repeat everything
to be the most likely to be under- & over- pitied

everyone's rolling suitcases to their childhood home
my great grandmother's mother

appeared in a dream as a fist
when I unfurled the rosebud tightness

my father's poop hole stretched unnaturally wide

I don't have enough friends to say
"I'm sorry, I have other plans"

I don't have enough friends to not instantly
reply to email

long absences in the absence of anything
soooooooooooooooo

worth it

when I get home to my father's house
I'm gonna invite my sister's work friends to pee sweetly in my pink eye!

"Sleepies for gurls"
when we cannot sleep because of the horror!

my mother comes in holding up the rest of my family
& goos me into feeling

as with everything
I am lost inside the silver hologram that turns my world shiny

the horror of our displacement is a total
o yah situation

this guy's torso is the same length or longer
than his legs

the only way he's getting my money
is if he poses

cars stop in the street and shout
the long history of my family at me

my grandmother's garden where my mother's father
recited ancient lyrics for crabsticks

her butterfly tits have a lotta flair
when I get up close to those wings
I go o wow o wow
o woww o wowwwww
o wowwwwwwwwwwwwwwwwwwww!

Instant Classic

O! how my back hurts
all this wasted life
shall I tally up the hours lost
shall I finally read Blake's illuminated poetry
if only I could spend a lifetime on a line
eat a freaking salad and turn it into
writing too ugly for the academy
what do you call someone who made nothing
out of years and years of opportunity?
O! I would focus more on the breath
but I love my country too much
you try way too hard to find out
which I'm referring to
so conscious of every minute
living so totally in the present
I leak blood memory and fade badly
is there some magic in knowing me?
did you not poison the garden of love
before you laughed like a captive
at my bad pronunciation
all the signs present
I could not shake off my origin
even school was useless

even going online with a new name
left me so completely exposed
the problem is the most exotic thing
I could do is suffer
& already I do

a little life / everyone's theme

what if someone could never get better
& someone else could never give up

The natural sunlight goes away

I ogle shit & ogle shit & ogle shit
stately promises and stately
destiny
                    I sweated and sweated and sweated

Shakespeare in the park
I wore my Sunday suit
Macbeth tore up my underwear
I piss thru my sticky pubes
in the laundry and in the wash
they come up in big magnificent clumps
                    I clap and I clap and I clap

I laughed and I laughed and I laughed
donald duck got chubby
we fluffed him & got sent home
I gotta say something if it's all right
with you
                    I waited and waited and waited

my sisters gave word to our mermaid mothers
we can be ***** when we can account for it
but I cannot account for the stray nodes
I ride horsey on very important accounts
we flay our lippy bodies on more bodies
                    I see you & I know you & I admire you
                    I see you & I know you & I admire you
                    I see you & I know you & I admire you

I will always see you
& I will always know you
& I will always admire you
& will never ask for more

Is there a way to drain a lake you are afraid you will one day drown in?

to prepare for all possible possibilities I must admit
I feel extra saggy
my cousin's husband gets married for a green card
but neither of them care about America at all
    well I do & I care about Korea too
& I care about China too
& I care about Pakistan too
& I care about the southern plains of Mongolia
& I care about the dwindling sheep
& I care about the big fat clouds of summer
& I care about other people who are living thru some shit
    on the car ride through the fields of broccoli trees I'm like
draw as you see it
and you are like I see it as just trees
and I am like brah-cah-lee
so brah, do you know much
about me?
so brah, do you feel like you could
really get me?
so brah, do you think this outdoor petting

is really that fun for me?
so brah, can I dangle this lampshade
like a hypnotist?
focault is all like I hate cauliflower on penises
and baudrillard is like ya
I hate simultaneous
orgaaaaaaaaaaaaaaaaaaaaaaaaassming!
& I swear to gahhhh everyone is like yep
me too
this yeppers won't give me a chance
to really gaze
into this still-draining cyst
I took a shower
and my ovaries were leaking everywhere
I was like this is truly the kewlest thing I've ever felt
& literally no one was there to make me feel seen
my cousin's husband is buzzing after a trip to southern China
"my goal is to eat an animal from every letter of the alphabet
except I can't figure out what to do about X"
"just eat an x-ray of some stupid animal and call it a freaking day"
"just eat some bag of unknown crap and call it X—"
I got super bored and started thinking about jewelry
Is there fashion in heaven?
What clothes will be available to me?
Do heavenly creatures have to choose an age?
What if I choose to be 17
and my mother chooses to be 17
and her mother chooses to be 17?
My father is like just go and eat something

Extra Yaaaaaaaammy
and I am all like guhh
I'm all like ummmmmmmmmmmmm
I'm all like soooooooooooooooooo
I'm all like ugghhhhhhhhhhhh
to think of heaven
to think of the future
I can't even contain all that
I thought was already here
I can't even remember all that
I had to say to those I cannot live without
& anyway I forget
& anyway I forget
& I forget
& I forget
& I forget
& I forget everything
& I have nothing much to say
& I can't promise anything
& I can't be full of boundless love
& I can't go into the shops searching for extra yaaaammy
but I feel full & awake
& I live here now
& what if I am good like this?
what if this is it

why do we have to all be someone

support me without ingesting me
I gotta go home to my family
I gotta eat bread with my fingers
and leave work early for more candy
more life more sad songs about
making it and losing everything
you don't gotta ask I always will
make myself available to yr pain
I will touch yr heart & look into yr eyes
if it calms u then pls pls pls
walk out with me into the light
everyone's waiting for me
to bring you to them

volition

ooh yes
connecting instead of
controlling

under the chiming bell

in the lower piney creek valley
I learn to move as ghosts do
after thirty five years of belching
I finally qualify as a trophy
in the woods I am mostly small
~ insignificant ~
in love with nothing and no one
boredom is a kind of armor
capitalism no longer contagious
seeing with my own eyes
each raindrop ceasing to exist
still I fear birth as much as death
the non-consent of existence
will never be resolved in no lifetime
has anyone ever lived
through someone else's ending
or just me?
so weird being allowed to enter
not as a servant
but as a guest
the crudeness of patronage
all those childhood prayers
wasted essentially

in the end I was not too beautiful for this
failed to be much of an exception at all
at least I can still dream
to possess the kind of face
often inscribed into archways
mid-scream like a gargoyle with nothing
better to do
the holy don't need us
wretches of a different order
looking for someone or nothing
I was supposed to be staff
then everything changed
and it didn't even matter I was born wrong
will someone tell someone who I am
will someone please please tell me

YOUR PROBLEMS

it was enough to be capable of dreaming

every time someone peed I bled pinkly

the ceremony was contingent on buying off the registry

guess I am against the wh*te s*pr*m*c*st c*p*t*l*st p*tr**rchy

I I I I I I IIIIII aaaaaaaaaaaaaaaaaaaaaaaaaaaaaa ya!

doiiiiioiiiiioiiiiiioiiiioiiii

my cunt hides in the cutest fashion

& does not signify anything

I'd like to decolonize but still I find myself

reverting back to body parts

gender is totally fucked and I'm completely wrong

it seems like everyone is insensitive to YOUR PROBLEMS

no one in the world has ever considered YOUR PROBLEMS

not one person has reacted appropriately to YOUR ISSUES

everyone is so quick to stigmatize YOUR CONCERNS

"I'm bored of your apocalyptic obsessions"

"did I love too much"

seriously, it doesn't matter

the only time I ever mattered

was on my baby first birthday

when I didn't have any problems

and everything was still to come

IT WAS SO BRIGHT I COULD NOT SEE

RUNNING JUST TO MOVE

I WANTED TO SEE ROETHKE'S POOL

COULD HAVE BEEN ANYWHERE

FACEDOWN WAS A ROMANTIC DETAIL

TRIED TO BE UNWELL TOGETHER

WE DIDN'T HAVE MONEY

WE DRANK VERY SMALL CUPS OF WATER

ONE AFTER ANOTHER

SHE DUG OUT QUARTER

AND I LEFT THREE DIMES AND A NICKEL

AMERICAN MONEY CONVERTS BADLY

I DRAGGED MY SUITCASE ONTO THE BUS

RAN THROUGH BLINDING LIGHT

IT WAS SO BRIGHT I COULD NOT SEE

BUT I SEARCHED THE LEFT-BEHIND BOOKS

I'VE LOOKED FOR MEANING

I'VE GIVEN UP ON LOVE

PLOTTED OUT THE ENTIRETY OF A LIFE

STUDIED THE ESOTERIC MASTERS

LET THEM TOUCH ME WITH THEIR DISEASED MOUTHS

IF ONLY THERE WAS SOMEWHERE TO GO

A SANATORIUM FOR THE ALMOST-INSANE

AS TIME PASSED I MELLOWED OUT

BUT STILL I AM FASCINATED WITH FLOATING

FACE DOWN ARMS OUT HAIR THINNED

GOING ALL THE WAY BACK TO THE BEGINNING

THERE WAS WATER BETWEEN US

AND I ASKED YOU TO REACH OUT

AND TOUCH ME RIGHT THERE . . .

YES THERE

Acknowledgments

The following poems are co-authored by my friends:
  "ariana's theme," "ariana's theme (reprise)," "it brought you," "remember /
  it brought you (reprise)" by Ariana Lenarsky
  "tanaïs's theme" by Tanaïs
  "jenny's trying/ victoria's theme" by Victoria Ruiz
  "brittani's theme" by Brittani Nichols
  "IT WAS SO BRIGHT I COULD NOT SEE" by Adrian Randall

I am so grateful for their words and their generosity in allowing me to
share them.

Earlier versions of poems were published in: *Adult, BOMB, Coconut,*
ESPNW, Everyday Genius, The Hairpin, HTMLGiant, Los Angeles Review
of Books, The New Republic, New York Times, O'clock Press, PEN America,
Pinwheel Journal, Poetry, Prelude, Sink Review, Third Rail Quarterly, The
Volta, and *West 10th Journal.*

Portions of this book were written while in residency at Shakespeare and
Company Bookstore in Paris, Summer Literary Seminars in Vilnius, the
Lower Manhattan Cultural Council, Yaddo, and Jentel.

"it's spring" references "Ode to Joy" by Frank O'Hara.

"It was a period when cunt was in the air" references *Quiet Days in Clichy* by
Henry Miller.

"HAMMER" references the ESPN documentary *The Price of Gold*.

"We must rapidly begin" references Martin Luther King Jr.'s "Beyond Vietnam" speech.

Thank you to the artist Li Shixiong for the cover art.

Much gratitude to my agent Samantha Shea, my editor Tony Perez, as well as Elizabeth DeMeo, Jakob Vala, Molly Templeton, and everyone at Tin House Books for making this book with me.

The title of this book comes from a poet I love and whom I am forever grateful to—my mother.

Finally, eternal thanks to all my family and friends. This is because of you.